AUGUSTA READ THOMAS

D0504042

TRACES

FOR PIANO

ED 4442
First Printing: September 2010

ISBN 978-1-4234-9609-0

G. SCHIRMER, Inc.

DISTRIBUTED BY
HAL•LEONARD® CORPORATION
7777 W. BLUEMOUND RD. P.O. BOX 13819 MILWAUKEE, WI 53213

"Traces" for solo piano, composed in 2006, was commissioned by the Montalvo Festival for Lang Lang.
The World Premiere took place on 26 January 2009, in Baltimore,
on the Evolution Contemporary Music Series (at An Die Musik)
by Amy Briggs, pianist.

It is preferred, but not required that a pianist would play all five Traces at once.

The idea was to take the distant perfumes of other musical idioms
(and it should be noted that there are no quotes of music by other composers in Traces)
and to imagine what it would be like to cross-fertilize them.
What would J.S. Bach crossed with BeBop sound like?
How would Scarlatti's Baroque Ornamentation crossed with Art Tatum sound?

These works took me countless months to compose. They were fun, challenging and exhilarating to create.
I composed them at a piano, note by note, playing the music at a super slow tempo over and over again.
(Impromptu is an expansion of my Piano Etude #6.)

The work is dedicated to Amy Briggs.
The composer expresses her gratitude to Makiko Hirata.

Composer's Note:

"My works are organic and, at every level, concerned with transformations and connections. While my music is highly notated, precise, carefully structured, thoughtfully proportioned and so forth... and although the pianist is playing from a very specific text, I like my music to have the feeling that it is organically being self-propelled - on the spot! As if we listeners, the audience, are overhearing a captured improvisation.

I like my music to be played so that the "inner-life" of the different rhythmic syntaxes is specific, with characterized phrasing of the colors, harmonies, and the like - keeping it ultra alive – such that it always sounds spontaneous.

For their sublime, precision and technical mastery, I deeply thank pianists who play TRACES in this fashion."

—Augusta Read Thomas

A recording by Amy Briggs is available on
ARTCD20002007

dedicated with admiration and gratitude to Amy Briggs

TRACES
for solo Piano

Augusta Read Thomas
(2006)

I. Reverie

Like Robert Schumann (The Poet Speaks) crossed with George Crumb

Spiritual and resonant ♩ = 40 or slower; a dreamy timeless space

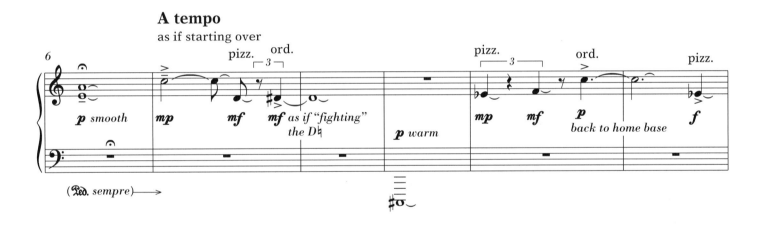

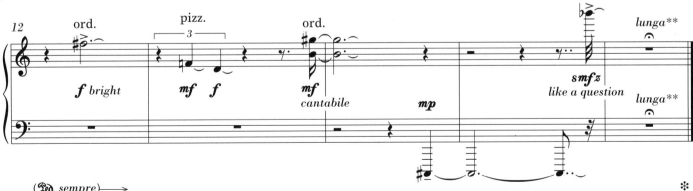

* "Pizz." means to pluck the string, inside the piano, with fingernail. This is cancelled by "ord". When re-plucking
a note, try *not* to dampen the already-ringing resonance.

** Final fermata must be at least 15 seconds long.

II. Caprice

Like Scarlatti's Baroque Ornamentation crossed with Art Tatum

♩ = 60–66, as fast as possible, and the tempo can fluctuate as needed

Note: Grace notes come before the beat and are supposed to "mess up" the pulse, such that what follows them is slightly late. They should be slow enough to be heard and never be slid nor rushed through.

three fermatas are like
playful question marks

* Trill from slow to fast.

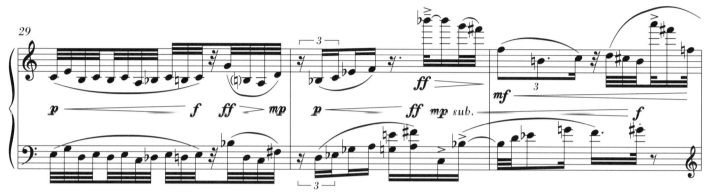

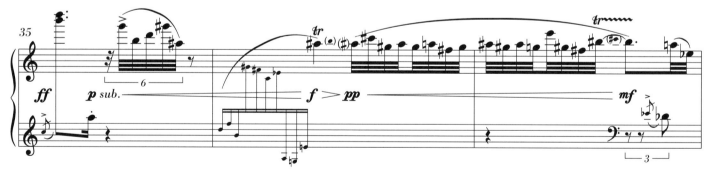

rit. freely   accel. freely   a tempo

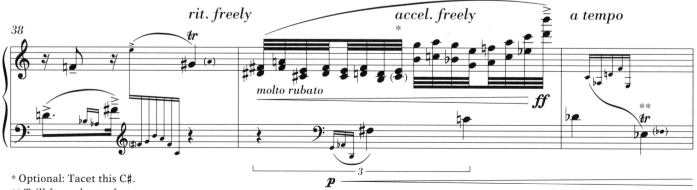

* Optional: Tacet this C♯.

** Trill from slow to fast.

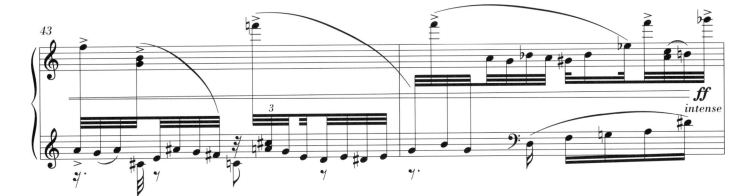

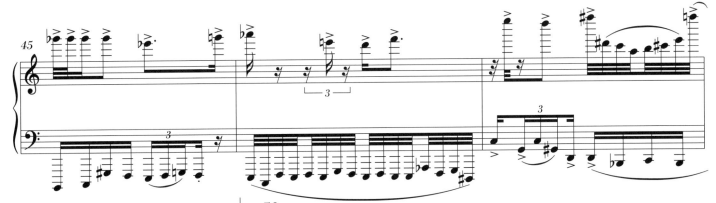

*From here to the end of the movement should be felt and shaped as one long phrase.

III. Tango
Like Astor Piazzolla crossed with John Coltrane

Playful and spirited ♩ = 92–108; vary tempo freely

slinky, and like an interruption

slight rit.   *a tempo*

jazzy and tango-like

* Trill from slow to fast.   *similar to measure 5 ("slinky")*

Note: Every fermata should sound like it is the end of the piece, such that what follows is a kind of "surprise".
After every fermata, an immediate *a tempo* is desired.

slight rit.

a tempo

Insistent

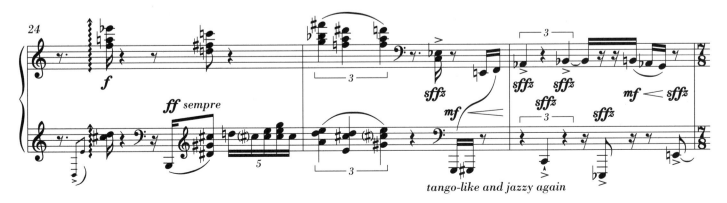

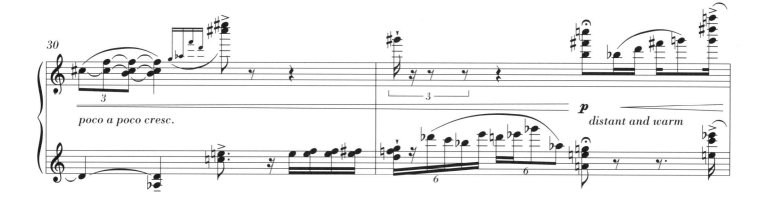

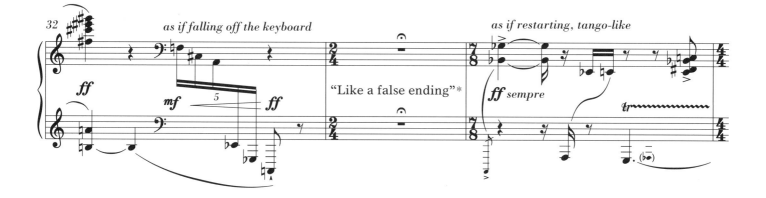

*Note: It is okay to end the movement here at the discretion of the player.

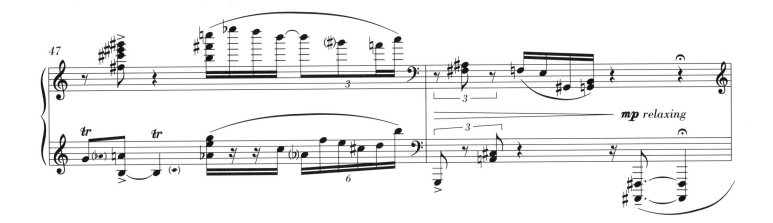

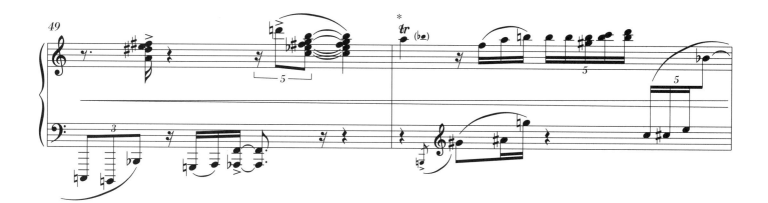

ritard freely

Like a false ending

a tempo

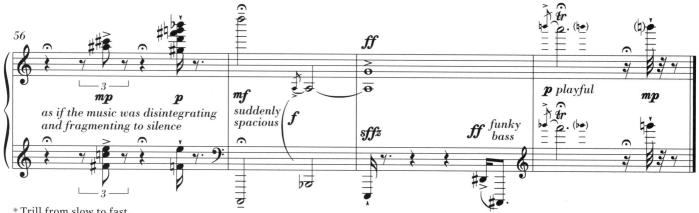

as if the music was disintegrating and fragmenting to silence

* Trill from slow to fast.

IV. Impromptu

Like Thelonious Monk crossed with Chopin

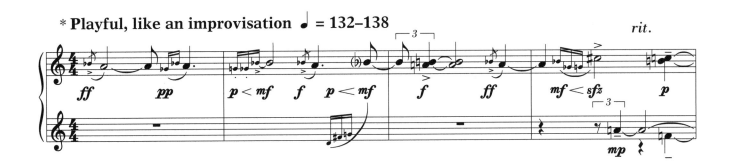

*Conversational in spirit; like different voices speaking to one another from various distances; richly dimensional.
Bar 1 through 20 can be played 15% slower but the tempo relationships should be maintained.

12

♩ = 112–120

Middle Ped.

(Mid. Ped.)

Middle Ped.

Middle Ped.   ✳

Middle Ped.   ✳   Middle Ped.   ✳

14

♩ = 120, or As fast as possible, and variable*

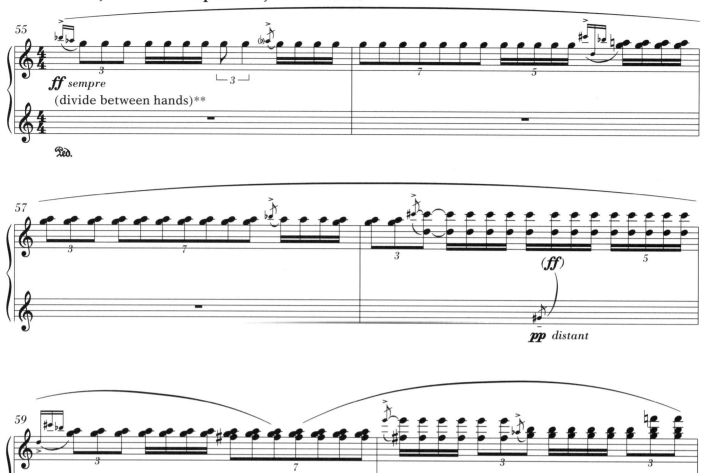

*The tempo **should** be variable and does **not** have to be stable from measure to measure, adding to the "twittering" and "jazzy" effect.
The rhythms should be played *rubato a piacere*.

**Note: It is intended that each pianist must divide between the two hands all the repeated notes in the manner they most prefer.
This is for a particular color as well as for the tempo(s).

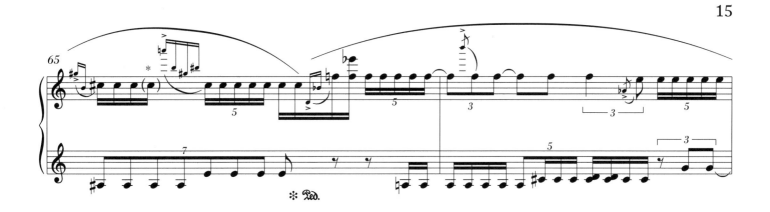

*Optional: Tacet this C♯.

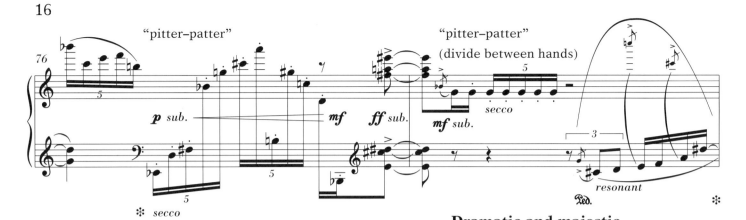

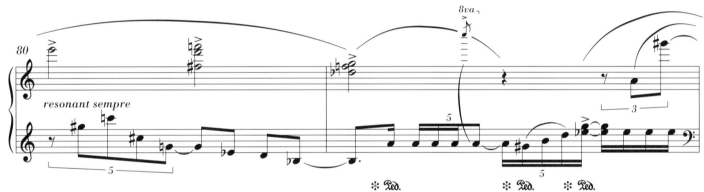

Dramatic and majestic for 13 beats

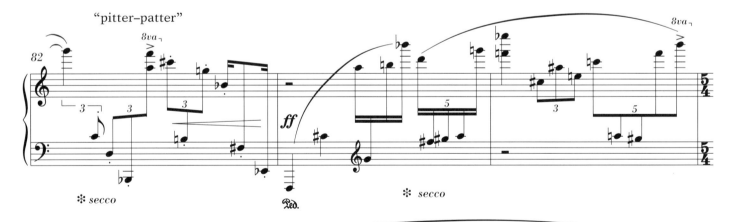

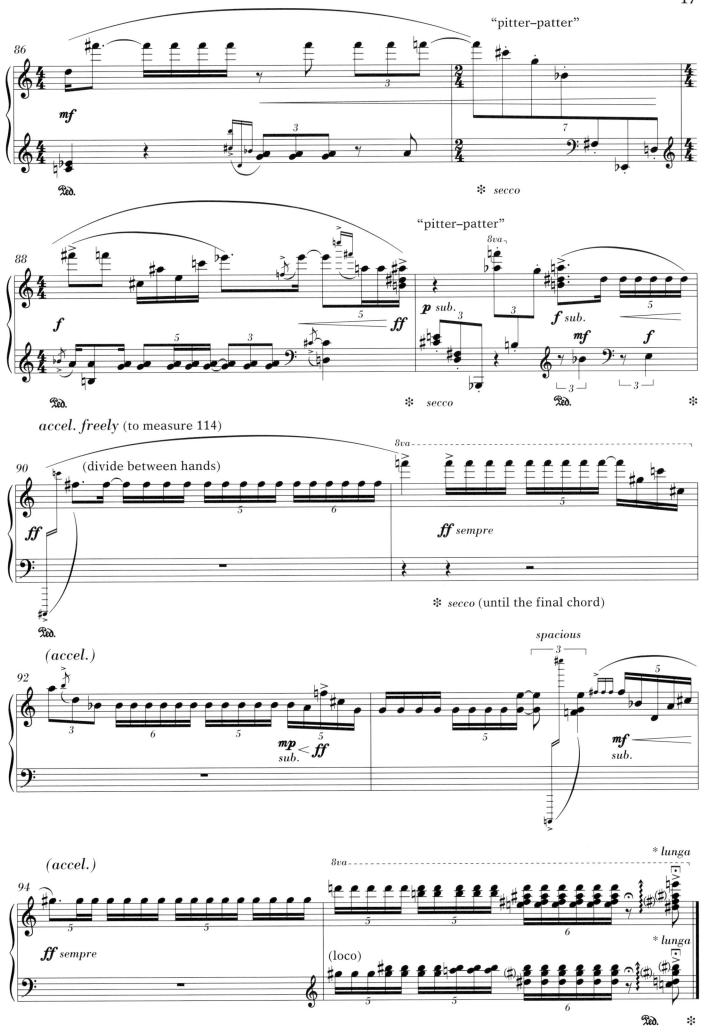

*Circa 10-12 seconds

V. Toccata

Like J.S.Bach crossed with BeBop

♩ = 60 or as fast as possible, **if you can play it even faster**

f *sempre with slight dynamic nuances at the discretion of the player, which are needed to delineate the macro and micro phrases as well as to articulate clearly the music of the extreme registers.*

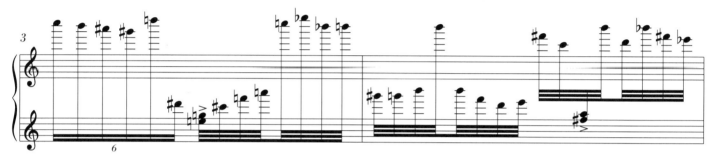

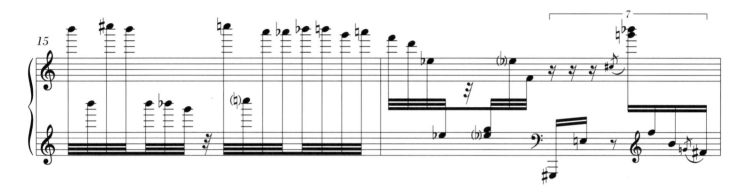

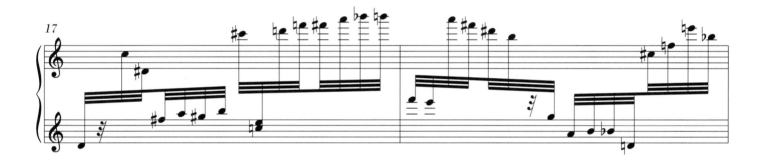

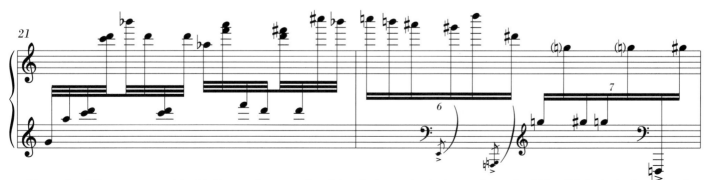

* Every chord (2 or more notes) in this Toccata is accented and, in relation to the single-note lines, should be slightly in the foreground, such that the two layers take on an interesting dimensionality.

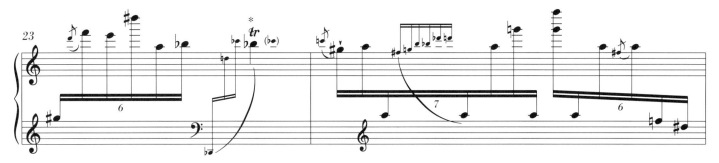

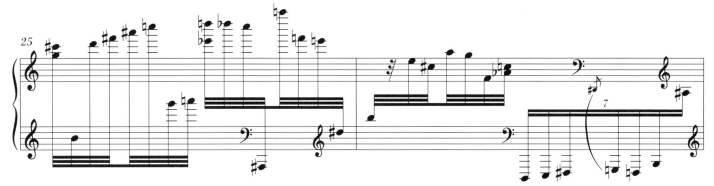

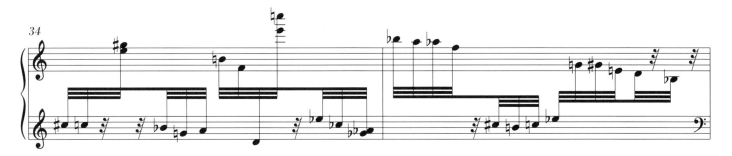

* Every trill in this Toccata should accelerate, pushing with momentum into the music that follows it.

* See note on page 20.

poco rit. (through m. 59)

accel. to end, driving
forward with force

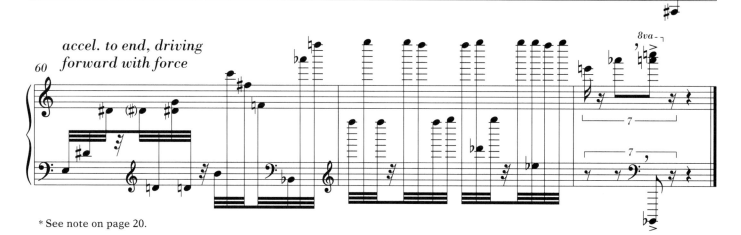

* See note on page 20.